Developing Life-long Readers

Margaret Mooney

Learning Media
Wellington

Contents

Knowing About Reading

"I haven't got a home-reader tonight. We didn't do reading today."

A bell knolling for yet another day when the education system missed out? Or, music praising an enlightened school where reading is an integral part of the entire day, and the readers are the children?

Teachers have always been concerned with the materials and methods used in the teaching of reading. However, during the past two decades, New Zealand teachers, parents, and the wider community have worked together in the evolution of a set of beliefs which places more emphasis on the "why" and "how" of literacy learning, rather than just the "what" and "when" of reading or writing. Thus, the child's exclamation above is not necessarily a spilling of the beans on a teacher's failing but, we hope, a reflection of a programme based on the following beliefs:

Reading programmes should be child centred.
Reading for meaning is paramount.
Reading must always be rewarding.
Children learn to read by reading.
Children learn best on books that have meaning and are rewarding.
The best approach to teaching reading is a combination of approaches.
The best cure for reading failure is good first teaching.
The foundations of literacy are laid in the early years.*

These beliefs reflect our understanding of how we can help children become life-long readers and writers. Reading is no longer seen as only a set of skills needed to decode the printed word, but as receiving and giving messages through creating one's own texts as well as recreating and extending one's horizons from messages recorded by others. Similarly, the teacher is no longer the sole instructor working through a predetermined set of activities. The teacher is one who shares responsibility and response ability with the learner. Thus, the teacher becomes a facilitator and respondent, ever mindful that true readers and writers are "self-winding" and choose to read and write well beyond the care and guidance of the school system.

---

* *Reading in Junior Classes.* Department of Education, Wellington. 1985, p. 9.

1

Each belief is considered briefly.

Reading Programmes Should be Child Centred

A child-centred programme is more concerned with how children learn, and with helping children to learn how to learn, than with instructing.

This requires a shift in focus from the traditional concern with imparting knowledge to ensuring that the conditions that have fostered and nurtured natural learning during the child's early years are the foundation of the school environment. These conditions focus on the child as the learner, and not on the adult as the teacher. The learning has occurred and been accepted as a natural part of living. All attempts have been accepted without strings attached.

A child-centred programme begins with what a child can do and decides on the next appropriate learning opportunities, rather than with considering what has been taught and simply providing more knowledge.

A child-centred approach reflects the saying "A child is not a vase to be filled but a fire to be lit." The teacher's role is to awaken the interest and power within children to enable the fire to be lit, and to enable children to become aware of what they already know, are able to do, what they need to know, and where they can get the appropriate help.

Reading for Meaning is Paramount

The emphasis on the development of a child's understanding and thinking, rather than solely on the acquisition of knowledge, brings an even greater focus on meaning as a part of learning. A reader does not read in order to then get meaning; a reader brings meaning to and gains meaning whilst reading. In other words, comprehension is part of the act of reading and not an exercise that follows.

If beginning readers are to develop an attitude of reading with meaning, the books children meet should impart messages to them. They should be written from a child's point of view, and the meaning should be directly accessible to the reader and not dependent on the teacher or parent for interpretation. Further readings reveal deeper or alternative meanings which may lead the reader to reconsider the meaning gained from the first encounter with the text.

Readers and writers construct meaning through interaction between what is in their head and what is on the page.

Reading Must Always be Rewarding

Constructing meaning enables the reader to discover that books have the power to delight, amuse, comfort, challenge, satisfy, and dismay. These rewards, along with the satisfaction of knowing one can interact with the author in this way, provide motivation for further effort and success. Readers read because they find satisfaction in reading and what reading does for them.

If we are serious about developing life-long readers, we need to ensure that our children discover and experience the rewards of reading by means of reading itself. This also means that rewards within the class programme should be for the "behaviour of learning" rather than for "learned behaviour". For example, ticks or stamps on a page of follow-up activities reward learned behaviour and, in time, will make the child dependent on the teacher's approval. Acknowledging efforts to use appropriate strategies, on the other hand, rewards the behaviour of learning. Choosing to read, enjoying reading, and being able to respond—all bring their own rewards and motivate further reading.

Children Learn to Read by Reading

Reading to gain meaning, and experiencing the rewards of reading, can only be learnt by reading. Children do not learn to read in order to be able to read a book, they learn to read by reading books. The attitudes and behaviours acquired from first experiences with books should confirm the child's desire and ability to be a reader. The models adults provide show reading as a purposeful and whole act, and these are the aspects that children first try to emulate. Perfecting any one part comes later.

The "wholeness" of reading can only be understood and become part of a reader's strategy when meaning is paramount and the learner is given opportunity to create and recreate stories that reflect

3

and enrich his or her life. A beginning reader uses exactly the same process as a skilled reader, in the way that a slow-progress reader uses the same process as a high-progress reader. The only difference between them is how well each uses the process.

Children Learn Best on Books that are Rewarding and Have Meaning

Books that are worth reading and that enhance the children's view of themselves as readers will convince them that reading is worthwhile and satisfying, and that it is for them. The books used in reading programmes should be the best books available; books which have special meaning for each particular child and group of children, and which help them understand more about themselves and their world.

When selecting books for use in reading programmes, teachers could consider the following:*

Does the story have charm, magic, impact, and appeal?

Will the child demand that the book be reread, or will they revisit it by themselves?
Will chunks of language and meaning resurface at later times?
What is the book's lasting appeal?
Will the book stand repeated readings?

Is the idea worthwhile?

Does the author's message have merit for its own sake?
(Many stories contain a moral, but morals should be inherent in the story and not presented as a reason for the reading.)
Is the idea worth the time and effort spent on the reading?
Does the story say something new, or, if a familiar theme, does it offer a new view?

Is the story's shape and structure appropriate?

Does the shape and structure help to carry the reader through the story?
Does the story have a beginning, a middle, and an identifiable climax with an acceptable resolution?

---

* These criteria were developed by the New Zealand Department of Education for use in the selection and trialling of scripts for the *Ready to Read* series.

Does the story create its own pace?
How has the author linked the episodes?
What gaps is the reader required to fill?
How does the author signal a change of pace, mood, or action?

Is the language effective?

Does the language suit the theme and the characters?
Does the language spark the child's imagination, and inspire thought?
Are there memorable phrases and/or sentences?
Do the characters act and speak naturally?
Does the author use book language to heighten the story's shape?
How much does the author leave to the reader's imagination?

Is the story authentic?

Is the story credible to the reader?
Does it avoid condescensions, stereotyping, and inaccuracy?
Does the author fulfil the promises engendered by the title, theme, and story shape?
Will it lead the child into further reading and learning?

Do the illustrations help the reader gain meaning from the text?

Are they appropriate for the theme and characters?
Do they make the meaning of the text clearer?
Do the illustrations reflect the mood of the story and give rise to feelings and emotions?
Do they complement the text, rather than compete with it?

Is the format of the book appropriate?

Do the book's size and its shape suit the content and the reader, or do they merely fit a series format?
Do the typeface and size, spacing, and line breaks match the reader's stage of reading development?

The Best Approach to Teaching Reading is a Combination of Approaches

At an early age, children learn that talk is used to express needs and feelings and to share information. Children learn to talk because they see people talking to them and with them, and they become aware that they are expected to talk themselves. The rewards of having learnt to express their needs and feelings through sound spur the children on to more learning and refining, and to discovering new ways in which talk can help them grasp and convey meanings. This further learning is continuously supported by others talking to and with the children and providing opportunities for the children to talk by themselves.

So it is with reading. Children's efforts in learning to read are greatly enhanced when there is reading to children, reading with children, and when children have opportunity to read by themselves. At the same time and in the same way, the children are also learning to write and to extend the ways in which they make sense of their experiences. The teaching approaches of shared reading, reading to children, language experience, guided reading, and independent reading used in classroom language programmes build on and extend the "to", "with", and "by" strategies that helped children to learn to talk. (Each of these approaches is considered later in this booklet and in detail in *Reading in Junior Classes*, the handbook of the *Ready to Read* series.)*

No single approach is sufficient for any child, nor is any predetermined combination of approaches. Mixing and matching will occur within any one day and within any one part of a day, according to the children's attitudes and abilities, the purpose of the reading, and the materials used.

The Best Cure for Reading Failure is Good First Teaching

Achieving a successful balance of materials and approaches depends on a perceptive and caring teacher. Good first teaching requires a responsive approach where the teacher is aware of what the child can do, what situations will be appropriate to assist the child to meet the next challenges, and what support will be needed. Responsive teaching ensures each step is secure enough to be a springboard for the next learning and that the learner has the resources and confidence for success.

---

* *Ready to Read* has been developed and published by the New Zealand Department of Education for the teaching of reading in junior classes.

Understanding the learning and reading processes and being familiar with the materials available are as important as knowing the children in one's care. Good teaching can only occur when all three are operating harmoniously.

The Foundations of Literacy are Laid in the Early Years

By the time children enter school, they have already acquired many attitudes and understandings about language and have well established learning processes in many areas. Five or six years of learning, using, and refining in several language areas (especially speaking, listening, moving, and viewing) have developed an expectation of meaning. They are well on the way to learning to make sense of their world. Their view of the world and their way of responding to it differs from child to child according to their culture and experiences. However, all have experienced success in learning, and it is the school's task to ensure that this learning forms the foundation for further learning, and that learning to read and write is as natural and successful as learning to walk or talk.

Knowing the Reader

When children feel that their own experiences are accepted, they become confident in transferring that learning process to new situations. They are eager to solve new problems and learn more about themselves and their world. This positive attitude enables children to approach books with keen anticipation. As they extend and refine their understandings about reading, they display new behaviours. The successful application of these results in a growth in attitude and increased understanding.

These attitudes, understandings, and behaviours can be grouped into three broad stages of reading development: emergent, early, and fluency. Some of the characteristics of readers at each stage are listed below. These characteristics are not included as checklists, nor are they definitive or exhaustive. It is most unlikely that any child will display all of the characteristics listed. It is likely, however, that each will show evidence of competence in some characteristics from more than one stage at any one time. Some of the attitudes, understandings, and behaviours of previous stages and levels will continue to be evident as children become more skilled. These become the launching pads for further learning.

The Emergent Stage

Attitudes

Is keen to hear and use new language.
Shows pleasure in the rhyme and rhythm of language.
Enjoys "playing" with language.
Is keen to listen to stories, rhymes, and poems.
Is keen to participate in stories, rhymes, and poems.
Expects books to amuse, delight, comfort, and excite.
Has an attitude of anticipation and expectancy about books and stories.
Expects to make sense of what is read to him/her and what he/she reads.
Is keen to return to some books.
Is keen to respond to some stories.
Wants to read and sees him/herself as a reader.
Is confident in making an attempt.
Responds to feedback.

Understandings

Knows language can be recorded and revisited.
Knows how stories and books work.
Thinks about what may happen and uses this to unfold the story.
Understands that the text, as well as the illustrations, carry the story.
Recognises book language and sometimes uses this in speech, re-tellings, writing, or play.
Understands the importance of background knowledge and uses this to get meaning.
Knows the rewards of reading and rereading.
Experiences success which drives the child on to further reading.
Is aware of some print conventions, especially those relevant to directionality, capital letters, and full stops.

"Plays" at reading.
Handles books confidently.
Interprets pictures.
Uses pictures to predict text.
Retells a known story in sequence.
Develops a memory for text.
Finger-points to locate specific words.
Focuses on word after word in sequence—finger, voice, and text match.
Focuses on some detail.
Identifies some words.
Hears sound sequence in words.
Uses some letter-sound links.
Reruns to regain meaning.
Explores new books.
Returns to favourite books.
Chooses to read independently at times.

The Early Stage

Attitudes

Is eager to listen to and to read longer stories.
Expects to be able to get meaning from text.
Is willing to work at getting meaning.
Sees reading as more than the words on the page.
Shows confidence in taking risks and making approximations, and sees these as a way of learning.
Is confident in sharing feelings about and responses to books.
Is eager to confirm success by reading favourite and new books.
Is keen to read to others.
Seeks feedback.

Understandings

Shows increasing knowledge of print conventions.
Associates sounds with letter clusters as well as individual letters.
Accepts miscues as a part of striving to get meaning.

Understands the importance of a self-improving system in developing oneself as a reader.

Understands how real and imaginary experiences influence the meaning gained from books.

Increases sight vocabulary rapidly.

Understands how much attention needs to be given to text to confirm predictions.

Behaviours

Makes greater use of context for predictions.

Makes more accurate predictions.

Selects and integrates appropriate strategies more frequently.

Uses pictures for checking rather than prediction.

Reads on as well as reruns to regain meaning.

Confirms by cross-checking to known items.

Chooses to read more frequently.

Copes with greater variety of genres and themes.

Copes with more characters, scene changes, and episodes.

Frequently explores books independently.

Builds up pace.

The Fluency Stage

Attitudes

Expects to take a more active part in interacting with the author's message.

Expects to meet challenges but is more confident of overcoming them.

Expects to discover new meanings on further readings.

Is eager to extend reading interests.

Is keen to take initiative in responding to books.

Expects others to consider his/her responses to books.

Does not expect to agree with everything that is read.

Sees books as providing answers to many questions.

Expects books to be a part of daily life and seeks time to read.

Understandings

Knows to focus on details of print only when meaning is lost.

Understands that taking risks and making approximations are an essential part of reading.

Is aware of a variety of genres and can identify elements.

Understands that authors and illustrators have individual voices and styles.

Understands how to adjust reading pace to accommodate purpose, style, and difficulty of material.

Knows how to use books to get information.

Knows how to use the library.

Behaviours

Samples text rather than focuses on every detail.

Uses increasing knowledge of letter clusters, affixes, roots, and compound words to confirm predictions.

Uses strategies of sampling, predicting, confirming, and self-correcting quickly, confidently, and independently.

Sets own purpose for reading.

Makes inferences from text and illustration.

Compares styles and forms.

Maintains meaning over longer and more complex structures.

Copes with longer time sequences.

Copes with more complex characters.

Copes with less predictable texts.

Chooses to read for pleasure as well as for information.

Summarises text for retelling.

Uses the table of contents.

Responds in various ways, including critically.

Knowing the Books

A child's progress through the various stages of reading development is enhanced when they are able to enjoy books "that are rewarding and have meaning". The plethora of books on the market and books already available in schools means teachers need to be able to identify those which have the best potential for helping children to become successful and satisfied readers. Each book needs to be considered for the supports and challenges it offers children.

However, teachers need to remember that the supports and challenges in any one book will differ from child to child and, for any one child, from time to time. This will affect which books they select and how they present them.

Therefore, teachers need to be very familiar with material used in their classroom.

1   Greedy Cat*

For example, a teacher planning to use *Greedy Cat* would assess the book's features in this way:

The book portrays themes familiar to the children; shopping, food, and cats as pets. This reduces the amount of scene setting required, enables the reading to get underway quickly, and helps children to use their background experience to unfold the story line. The familiar setting also assists here. This setting is specific to the home, neighbourhood, and shop of the story, yet it is general enough for all readers to feel it is familiar.

---

*Cowley, Joy. *Greedy Cat*. Ready to Read, Department of Education, Wellington. 1983.

Greedy Cat is a real story, with an identifiable beginning, middle, and ending. It helps children see how a story works. The strong story line carries the reader through the reading and motivates rereadings.

The structure of this story with its repeated refrain, repeated pattern, and the inherent rhythm, creates a pace which supports the reader and encourages anticipation. The combination of these elements, and Greedy Cat's obvious increase in size, help the reader predict the next episode and feel in control of the story. Each reading heightens the anticipation and expectation of success.

The text offers a balance of book and natural language. For example, "Mum went shopping and got some sausages" reflects how children would think and talk in play, while "Along came Greedy Cat" is a good example of book language that is appropriate for beginning readers.

The humour of the story also appeals to most young children and encourages rereading and spontaneous response. Its illustrations reflect the complete story line, as well as providing a sub-plot which encourages revisiting and motivates a deeper level of picture interpretation. The reader is taken into the author's and the illustrator's confidence on page 3 with "Look out Mum". This sets the scene for thought of going beyond the text and reading between the lines.

Mum went shopping
and got some sausages.
Along came Greedy Cat.
He looked in the shopping bag.
Gobble, gobble, gobble,
and that was the end of that.

The format of the book and its layout reflect the story line and its shape and pace. There is a complete episode on each double opening, until the "chocolate" incident, when a new text layout creates a change of pace in anticipation of Mum's intervention. The final three pages leave no doubt in the reader's mind about the climax, but at the same time, there is room for further thought about the fate of Greedy Cat.

A colour wheel* on the back of *Greedy Cat* provides guidance on the suggested level for each of the three main approaches of shared, guided, and independent reading. These should be considered as starting points, with the teacher assessing how many of the book's features would confirm the children's current level of development and how many would be acceptable challenges. This careful consideration will form the basis for planning the lesson and presenting the book.

2 *I Can Read†*

It is especially important for beginning readers to be helped to see their responsibility as a reader, and to provide material which confirms their success intrinsically. These considerations are features of *I Can Read*. A teacher's notes about this book might include some of the following points: The book presents positive messages about reading for children, teachers, and parents. Reading is seen as success-orientated, satisfying, worthwhile for sharing, and learnt by reading.

The book's familiar settings and characters reflect the child's most secure and supportive surroundings and relationships. The photographs used add realism, portraying body language mirroring the caring and sharing theme of the text. The repetitive structure of the text, with its gradual introduction of challenges, all of which are at the end of sentences and clearly portrayed in the photographs, ensures each page encourages the child to "try" the next page.

---

* Children's books published in the *Ready to Read* series carry a colour wheel on the back cover. Letters in the outer ring indicate the suggested approach (S for shared reading, G for guided reading, I for independent reading). Colours indicate the levels at which the material and approach may be suitable. The colours represent the three main stages of reading development as follows: magenta represents the emergent stage; red, yellow, dark blue, and green represent levels within the early stage; orange, blue, purple, and dark yellow represent levels within the fluency stage.

† Malcolm, Margaret. *I Can Read. Ready to Read*, Department of Education, Wellington. 1983.

The layout of each page is consistent throughout. Each unit of text and illustration is clearly distinguished, and it is clear which text belongs to which pictures. Spacing between words allows for finger-pointing, but does not lose a sentence pattern of word, space, word. In this case the children need to be able to read five spaces. Finger-pointing, as an aid to voice-word matching, is further aided by the text being high enough on the page for the children to be able to touch the text without their hand slipping off the page. Some children may have initial difficulties with "myself" as one word, and the teacher will need to be alert to see how the children meet this challenge.

The colour wheel indicates that many teachers may use this book for guided reading at the emergent level. It provides many opportunities for innovation, both in its structure and its theme. Providing opportunities for children to meet the same vocabulary and structure in different contexts and formats helps them learn about the constancy of text and thus establish understandings about and procedures for learning sight vocabulary.

I can read to myself!

3 My Bike*

Links between books within the series make the reader aware of how to use existing schema and knowledge to help them read new texts. Several examples of the support are among the features of *My Bike*.

The text reflects how a child learns to ride a bike, with each attempt being mastered and extended with further riding, and then riding in new areas, moving from the confines of the home or park to the open road and the seeking of new challenges. Many children will be able to identify with the theme, which is given further universality by the character's anonymity.

Its cumulative structure builds up reading power by increasing the amount of text with the repetition of previous achievements before introducing a new one. This also encourages the reader to carry the

* Martin, Craig. *My Bike*. *Ready to Read*, Department of Education, Wellington. 1982.

On Thursday, I rode my bike
around the trees,
over the bridge,
under the branches,
and through the puddle.

9

story line and sequence in their head, or to use previous pages for reference. The structure builds up pace, providing more impact for the drama of the short text on the last page and heightening the power of the climax. The contrast in the last two sections of text, and the climax itself, encourage further thought and questioning by the reader.

Days of the week provide the sequence structure (as well as providing links with *Our Teacher, Miss Pool*).* Pairs of prepositions help prediction and confirmation, and are clearly portrayed in the photographs. Some of the prepositions in this book are used in different context in *Nick's Glasses*,† where there is not the same text and illustration match.

* Cowley, Joy. *Our Teacher, Miss Pool. Ready to Read*, Department of Education, Wellington. 1984.
† Cachemaille, Christine. *Nick's Glasses. Ready to Read*, Department of Education, Wellington. 1982.

Four bare babies in a blackbird's nest.

4 *Blackbird's Nest**

The reader's efforts in developing a self-improving system are confirmed in books such as *Blackbird's Nest*.

This book presents non-fiction material, accurate in every detail of text and illustration, in a concise expository and artistic form. The story of one blackbird family offers a specific yet timeless view, capitalising on a child's natural curiosity about nature and life cycles. Outside and inside covers summarise the story line and define the purpose for reading.

The two elements of repetition create a support structure which is repeated in *The Wild Wet Wellington Wind*.† The framing of each page introduces the reader to the time gap between episodes, but these are linked through the repetition and the predictable story line.

Blackbirds fed,
  Blackbirds fed,
Blackbirds fed in a blackbird's nest.

The text provides for confirmation of predictions through using letter-sound associations of initial letters or consonant blends within the same page, or word endings, such as:

babies, bare, blackbird's
flew, grew
blackbird, blackbirds, blackbird's.

A change of tense for the final page forces a change of pace for the inferential and rather pensive ending.

* Harvey, Olive. *Blackbird's Nest. Ready to Read*, Department of Education, Wellington. 1982.
† Cowley, Joy. *The Wild Wet Wellington Wind. Ready to Read*, Department of Education, Wellington. 1986.

5   Night is a Blanket*

Teachers considering *Night is a Blanket* will find the seventy-two page miscellany offers many opportunities for readers to make comparisons between types, forms, and styles within the book, with others in the *Ready to Read* series, and with other material.

"The Story of Rona" and "Why the Moon has Shadows on her Face" are legends presenting different views of the same theme. Other viewpoints and forms of expression are portrayed in the illustration following each story. Further comparisons about the structure of legends and a contrast of themes could be made with *Maui and the Sun,*† a single title in the *Ready to Read* series. And further contrasts of theme and form are offered in the photographs of "The Night Sky" and "A Walk on the Moon", the illustration and text of "The Night was Dark and Stormy", and the music and verse of "E Ko, E Ko" and "Morning Chorus".

The variety of genres also ensures readers establish a purpose for reading and a pace appropriate for each item. For example, the story within a story in "Night is a Blanket" requires a more thoughtful and inferential approach than does "Washing Lines" or the more active reading of the play in verse, "Three Little Billy-goats".

Night is a Blanket and the other miscellanies are ideal for children to browse through, dipping and delving, either by themselves or with others. Miscellanies are also very suitable for teachers and children to read and talk about in shared and guided reading. Consider these collections as a potpourri for frequent revisiting and a springboard for other reading and writing.

Looking at books in this way enables teachers to select materials which confirm children's attitudes and competencies, and to provide books offering manageable challenges that ensure continued development as a reader.

---

* *Night is a Blanket*. *Ready to Read*, Department of Education, Wellington. 1986.
† Melser, June. *Maui and the Sun*. *Ready to Read*, Department of Education, Wellington. 1985.

Rona took a taha
and set off to get some water
from the spring.
The path to the spring was bumpy,
but Marama's light helped Rona
to see where she was going.

Suddenly, Marama went behind a cloud.
"Marama! Marama!" Rona shouted.
"Come out from behind that cloud!"
But Marama wouldn't come out.
Rona couldn't see the path any more.
She tripped
on the root of a ngaio tree.
Rona was angry with Marama
for hiding his light.
"See what you've done!"
she shouted.

The moon's light was still shining,
although there were shadows
on her face.

And when the people of Takei's village
look at the moon and see her shadows,
they remember the trap
that could not destroy moonlight.

Presenting the Book

Knowing the children and knowing the book helps a teacher decide on the purpose and approach most suitable for a particular reading. Teachers need to be aware that their role in helping children see themselves as life-long and successful readers differs according to the approach they select. Reading to, with, and by children each offer unique opportunities for the teacher to increase the children's confidence as readers and writers, and to help them take greater responsibility for their own learning.

The same book will require different approaches for different children. It is also likely that aspects of different approaches will be used within any one lesson. The balancing of "to", "with", and "by" (shared, guided, and independent reading) should depend on how much support the children need to be able to understand the author's idea, and how much responsibility they are able to take to confirm and extend themselves as readers.

Some publishers provide guidance on suggested levels. This information is only a guide, however, and teachers will need to confirm or amend it, and decide how to present material which does not have any such indication, by asking questions such as:

- Why do I want to use this book with these children?
- How much background knowledge and experience can the children bring to the reading? How much scene-setting will be required?
- Which of the book's features do I expect to be challenges, and which will provide support for the children?

How is the Balance Achieved?

If there are more challenges than supports, the book should probably be read to the children, or perhaps left until a later stage in their reading development.

If the balance is even, sharing the book may be appropriate. If there are more supports than challenges, the children and the teacher could read and talk and think their way through the book via guided reading.

If there are many more supports than challenges, the book could be read independently by the child.

Reading to Children

When reading to children, the teacher acts on behalf of the author, presenting the writing with as much enthusiasm and commitment as if it were his or her own. The teacher is the vehicle for the book's voice, enabling the children to interact with the author's central idea without having to interpret the written symbols.

The images are recreated in each child's mind according to their existing experience, knowledge, and cultural understanding which together combine to provide a "sponge" for the new ideas and visions. Each child's "sponge" will absorb different images and ideas. Whilst the absorption process is part of any reading, this approach is the only one where it is solely dependent on the teacher's presentation.

The teacher's role, therefore, includes presenting a wide variety of types, forms, and styles of writing and illustration. This should not be haphazard, and it is suggested that the teacher keeps a record of material read to the children, and of their responses.

Teachers should see reading to children as a continuing opportunity to extend children's horizons about books and to stimulate a desire to be a reader.

Shared Reading*

Showing children what reading can do for them and how they can be a reader, encouraging them to participate in readings, and being responsive to their efforts are key factors of the teacher's role in shared reading.

The teacher achieves these objectives by enticing the children to feel that they are co-writers with the author and co-readers with the teacher. Careful selection of material, the absence of any overt expec-

* See *Reading in Junior Classes.* Department of Education, Wellington. 1985. pp. 57–61.

tations or standards, and an enthusiastic presentation of the material will ensure that children see how the story works and will consider themselves in the author's chair as they carry the plot forward. At the same time, they will see themselves as readers as they unfold the story line and predict events and actions.

The experience is satisfying for the child, with intrinsic rewards from the reading confirming them as a reader and providing motivation for further involvement and reading. These readings will probably be dependent on some continued assistance from the teacher but, in time, most children will choose to read some stories independently. The teacher's task then becomes one of providing continued access to books and time for reading and responding.

Presenting a variety of structures through the shared reading approach develops an attitude of familiarity and expectation about the elements of the various genres. This leads to children becoming confident about taking more responsibility for the readings and for using them as models in writing and other language modes.

Guided Reading*

One of the teacher's main tasks in guided reading lies in ensuring that the child meets success as a "self-winding" reader. The teacher's role changes from acting on behalf of the author and demonstrating how a reader processes print to gain meaning (as in reading to children and shared reading), to one of encouraging each child to take control of the first reading and the unfolding of the story line. Children are responsible for making their own connection with the author through the text.

Allowing readers to take responsibility for the reading requires responsive teaching which helps a reader find out how to overcome challenges rather than just helping him/her to meet them. When a child is shown how to cope with a challenge, the focus is on learning behaviour that will support other learning. Responsive teaching is dependent on the teacher understanding and observing the reading process, that is, the act of comprehension, in action. Focusing on results is concerned only with *learned* behaviour.

* See *Reading in Junior Classes*. Department of Education, Wellington. 1985. pp. 69–75.

Focus on *learning* behaviour shows the learner how to be in control of the learning, how to transfer that learning, and how to build on it to ensure continued success and development.

Focus on learning behaviour requires the teacher to be constantly aware of what strategies of sampling, predicting, confirming, and self-correcting the child is using in order to gain meaning. When a reader loses the meaning, he or she should not be given an instant answer. This takes the responsibility away from the reader and, in time, makes them dependent on the teacher every time a difficulty is met. The teacher should give the reader time to employ known strategies and show the child how to regain meaning by looking for and using available cues. This ensures the responsibility remains with the reader, leading towards independent reading. The teacher guides the reader to the author's idea through the process rather than just through the story.

In other words, the teacher is concerned with empowering the child to be responsible and equipped for:

- initiating the reading;
- determining the purpose;
- being the author as well as the reader;
- operating at the level necessary to gain and maintain meaning;
- controlling input;
- employing coping strategies;
- experiencing success;
- initiating a response.

Language Experience*

The language experience approach provides an avenue for the teacher to talk, think, read, and write with the child or children, showing how ideas and experiences, both individual and shared, can be recorded for future reading and sharing. The children are thus involved in reading and writing as one process, highlighting the role of the reader and the author as creators of meaning.

---

* See *Reading in Junior Classes*. Department of Education, Wellington. 1985. pp. 61–9.

The teacher acts as a respondent and scribe for the author/s. This includes helping children respond to the ideas of others and to being part of a community of readers and writers. The teacher acts as an agent, helping children to value their own contributions, to see how others accept their ideas and writing, and to appreciate those of the other contributors.

Independent Reading*

One of the characteristics of a life-long reader is that they choose to read and enjoy doing so.

It is a habit that needs to be established early, and the teacher's role includes making independent reading an easy and attractive option at all times. This means that time needs to be set aside for the children to choose to read (completely separate from any set silent reading time), space must be available to relax while reading and sharing books, and there should be a wide selection of books. The range of books should both cater for the children's known interests and extend their horizons. There should be plenty of material for easy reading, and some that offers challenges.

The teacher's encouragement and interest in the books the children choose to read and share will reinforce the children's understanding that reading is worthwhile. The books chosen for reading, the children's responses to these, and the time and priority they allocate to reading, all provide teachers with valuable information about the children's attitudes, understandings, and reading behaviours, especially about the transfer of those evident during shared and guided reading situations.

Now the teacher needs to "stand back" and allow children to independently employ their repertoire of strategies. This provides the reader with confirmation that he/she is able to cope, and that these strategies can be refined as more texts are read and challenges met. Thus independent reading needs to be seen as one of the approaches which help children to read, and something which is necessary at

---

* See *Reading in Junior Classes*. Department of Education, Wellington. 1985. pp. 75–8.

every stage of reading development, rather than solely as a state for the skilled reader. The teacher's prime task is to make it possible for the reader to "hear" the author's voice directly, without outside help.

Encouraging Responses

It has already been stated that teachers need to concentrate on developing behaviours that foster learning and take children forward to meet the next challenge, rather than concern themselves with checking knowledge or skills learnt. Acceptance of this premise has implications for the reading "activities" provided in the classroom, especially any assigned following the reading of a book.

The following questions will help teachers clarify the purpose and nature of "activities" in their classroom and programmes:

- Do I provide activities to keep the rest of the children purposefully occupied so that I can devote more time to a single child or group?
- Do I provide activities to reinforce and extend what I've taught?
- Am I trying to provide opportunities for further dialogue between the reader and the author, and do I expect the reader to take responsibility for this?

Saying an unqualified "yes" to either of the first two questions will result in a completely different approach than would a "yes" to the third. The beliefs and principles conveyed in this book support the reader initiating the response.* In this case, the activities are not always determined by the teacher (or a publisher), do not emphasise checking completed learning, and cannot be assessed as correct/incorrect answers.

When the initiative is taken by the reader, their response:

- reflects what they determine to be of value and interest;
- is to the author and the author's idea rather than to set questions;

---

* Responses to the book are opportunities for the children to interpret the story in their own way, giving a sense of ownership of their experience of the author's idea.

- differs from reader to reader, and from time to time for any one reader;
- will vary according to the type and quality of the book read;
- may remain within the reader or may be expressed in any one of a variety of ways;
- may immediately follow the reading or may not be expressed for a considerable time;
- provides new contexts for further learning.

The teacher's role is to show readers how to respond to books and to provide time and space for children to contemplate, plan, and make their response. Sometimes, this will involve working with readers while they are responding—listening to their discussions and suggesting options for expressing their ideas and reactions. The teacher and the children would discuss how to determine the most appropriate response according to the book read, the reader's reactions, the purpose of the response, and the intended (if any) audience.

At other times, the teacher's role will include listening to, reading, viewing, and discussing the reader's response. The children need to understand that the teacher values their response and is interested in it. The teacher becomes the learner, discovering new things about the child, about reading, and the learning environment.

Knowing What's Happening

Response teaching, one of the key elements in a child-centred approach, is dependent on continuous appraisal of how the children act as "self-winding" readers and writers. This is reflected in the attitudes, understandings, and behaviours the readers display in expressing ideas, experiences, and feelings. They may do this through creating or retelling messages in a variety of forms through reading, writing, shaping, and speaking. This means that evaluation is part of the learning, and involves the learner's reading and writing to meet their own needs and desires.

Evaluation has more to do with knowing what is happening and how it is occurring, than with knowing what has happened. In other words, evaluation has more to do with the teacher knowing and accepting what the children use in their reading and writing, and understanding how they can be supported as they cope with the next challenges.

Knowing what's happening is dependent on knowing the children, knowing how children learn, making appropriate selections of materials and approaches, and observing and understanding the interdependence of these factors throughout the entire day.

Knowing what is happening means, for example, observing the use the children make of the book corner, the writing corner, or any of the other literacy-orientated features of the classroom; observing how they initiate and implement their own responses to books, events, or ideas; assessing their confidence and success in reading new and familiar texts or writing their own;* watching the ways they share their learning experiences and confirming each other as readers and writers.

Knowing what's happening means the teacher is a sharing member of the community each of whom finds reading and writing challenging, satisfying, and enjoyable.

Their fires have been lit and they will continue to burn!

---

* Taking running records is one way of obtaining accurate information on what occurs in the course of a reading. Guidance is provided by Marie Clay in *The Early Detection of Reading Difficulties*. Heinemann Educational Books 3rd ed., 1985. Also see *Reading in Junior Classes*. Department of Education, Wellington, 1985. Chapter 7.